Sanjeev K

NON VEGETARIAN
Snacks
&
STARTERS

Office Copy

Popular Prakashan Pvt. Ltd
Bangalore

Sanjeev Kapoor's
Any Time TEMPTATIONS SERIES
NON VEGETARIAN
Snacks
&
STARTERS

In association with Alyona Kapoor

Popular Prakashan

POPULAR PRAKASHAN PVT. LTD.
35-C, Pt. Madan Mohan Malaviya Marg
Tardeo, Mumbai-400 034.

© 2002 by Sanjeev Kapoor

First Published 2002

(3809)

ISBN - 81-7991-063-6

PRINTED IN INDIA
By Vakil and Sons Pvt. Ltd.,
Industry Manor, 2nd Floor,
Worli, Mumbai and Published by Ramdas Bhatkal
for Popular Prakashan Pvt. Ltd.
35-C, Pt. Madan Mohan Malaviya Marg,
Tardeo, Mumbai-400 034.

Dedication

This book is dedicated to
all the viewers of Khana Khazana
and my family and friends
who have been a constant support
to me at all times.

Note to the Readers

For me a starter would not only mean chicken *tikka* or *paneer pakora*. It would mean much more than that. For me a starter would be perfect when it tantalises the taste buds just enough so that the main meal can be relished later on. One could well smile at the thought because, more often than not, the starters end up being so filling that the main meal becomes merely a formality or even a waste!

This collection of non-vegetarian starters and snacks is as racy as a thriller. It is a part of the series of 'Any Time Temptations'. All the recipes have been picked out from my earlier books and segregated. We have a tongue tickling Tex Mex Chicken Wings which stands in contention with the internationally acclaimed *Tandoori Chicken* as also the extremely popular Chinese Crispy Wanton and Chilli Chicken.

For those who want a wholesome snack, the recipe of the traditional *Kheema Pav* will stand in good stead. Mincemeat is also made good use of in *Potli Samosa* and *Kheema* Frankie. If it's raining out there, make a cup of steaming hot tea and couple it with a plateful of delightfully different *Anda* and *Methi Pakoras*. The adventurous could probably try out the Chicken Gold Coin which has an appetising crust of sesame seeds.

Seafood lovers face a real dilemma choosing between delicious prawns and fish, fried or grilled, in our kingly list. *Amritsari Fish* would tempt any novice to try it out for the recipe is as easy as pie! If in the mood to dish up anything fancy, go for Crunchy Coriander Pomfret or the Open Steamed Dumplings.

All the recipes serve four portions and form part of a menu.

In case you would like to give ketchup the miss just this once, try out the various dips with the Cheese and Herb Dip being my personal choice. Enjoy and then ask for more...for starters and snacks like these deserve encores!

Acknowledgements

A. I. Kazi
Aditi Mehta
Afsheen Panjwani
Anand Bhandiwad
Anil Bhandari
Blue Cilantro, Mumbai
Brijesh Lohana
Capt. K. K. Lohana
Debasis Sikdar
Drs. Meena & Ram Prabhoo
Ganesh Pednekar
Grain of Salt, Kolkata
Harpal Singh Sokhi
Jaideep Chaubal
Jijesh Gangadharan
Jyotsna & Mayur Dvivedi
Lohana Khaandaan

Meghana Samant
Namrata & Sanjiv Bahl
Neelima Acharya
Neena Murdeshwar
Pooja & Rajeev Kapoor
Rajeev Matta
Rajneesh Sharma
Rutika Samtani
Shivani Ganesh
Smeeta Bhatkal
Sunit Purandare
Swapna Shinde
The Yellow Chilli, Jalandhar
The Yellow Chilli, Ludhiana
Tripta Bhagattjee
Uma Prabhu

CONTENTS

Tangdi Kabab	15
Murgh Ke Shami	18
Tex Mex Chicken Wings	20
Chettinaad Fried Chicken	22
Brandy Spiked Chicken	24
Chicken Satay	26
Andhra Chilli Chicken	29
Barbecued Chicken	31
Chilli Chicken	33
Chicken Flower Dumpling	35
Chicken Cutlet A L' Indienne	38
Anda Aur Methi Pakora	40
Chicken Gold Coin	42
Open Steamed Dumplings	44
Paper Wrapped Chicken	46
Kheema Pav	49
Chicken Tikka	51

Kheema Frankie	53
Crispy Chicken Wontons	55
Patrani Machchi	58
Golden Fried Jumbo Prawns	60
Grilled Fish Fingers	62
Amritsari Fish	64
Tandoori Pomfret	66
Prawn Balchao	68
Oriental Fish Kababs	70
Creole King Fish	72
Prawn Shaslik with Apple Curry Sauce	74
Chilli Fish Bhajji	78
Prawn Varuval	80
Dragon Sea Food Rolls	82
Samosa Potli	85
Crunchy Coriander Pomfret	88
Garlic Mustard Prawns	90
Chicken Burger	92
Farmhouse Lettuce Roll	94
Chicken Seekh Kabab	96

Mayonnaise 98
Sichuan Sauce 99
Coriander and Mint Chutney 101
Peanut Yogurt Dip 102
Chicken Stock 103

TANGDI KABAB

INGREDIENTS

Chicken drumsticks (chicken legs thigh section) 8	Gram flour (*besan*) .... 2 tbsps
Lemon juice .... 1 tbsp	Turmeric powder .... 1 tbsp
Ginger .... 1 inch piece	*Garam masala* powder .... 1 tsp
Garlic .... 6 cloves	Red chilli powder .... 1 tsp
Green chillies 4-6	Salt .... to taste
Skimmed milk yogurt .... 1 cup	*Chaat masala* powder .... 1 tsp
	Lemon wedges .... for garnishing

METHOD OF PREPARATION

1. Clean and trim excess fat and skin from the drumsticks. Dry them with a clean and absorbent kitchen towel. Make three to four long deep incisions. Apply lemon juice and keep aside.
2. Peel ginger and garlic, wash and grind them to a paste.

3. Wash green chillies, remove stems and then chop them fine.
4. Hang skimmed milk yogurt for fifteen to twenty minutes to drain off excess water.
5. Roast gram flour in a non-stick pan on low heat, stirring continuously. Cool and mix with hung yogurt, ginger and garlic paste, turmeric powder, *garam masala* powder, red chilli powder, salt and chopped green chillies.
6. Marinate chicken drumsticks in the above mixture and refrigerate for one to two hours.
7. Skewer marinated chicken drumsticks and roast in a moderately hot charcoal fired *tandoor* or alternatively cook in a pre-heated oven at 220°C for five minutes. Reduce oven temperature to 180°C and further cook for fifteen to twenty minutes or till completely cooked. Turn the drumsticks a couple of times to ensure even cooking and colour.
8. Serve hot sprinkled with *chaat masala* and lemon wedges.

Tangdi Kabab

MURGH KE SHAMI

INGREDIENTS

Chicken mince .... 600 gms.
Bengal gram split (*chana dal*) .....
.... ½ cup
Ginger .... 2 inch piece
Garlic .... 10 cloves
Onions .... 2 medium sized
Fresh coriander leaves .... 1½ tbsps
Fresh mint leaves .... 1½ tbsps
Lemon juice .... 2 tsps
Oil .... to fry

Cumin seeds .... ½ tsp
Coriander seeds .... ½ tsp
Peppercorns 5-6
Black cardamoms 3-4
Red chilli powder .... 1 tsp
Garam Masala powder .... ½ tsp
Mace & green cardamom powder
.... ½ tsp
Salt .... to taste

METHOD OF PREPARATION

1. Wash the *kheema* and drain out excess moisture. Soak *chana dal* for at least three hours.
2. Peel, wash and chop the ginger and garlic finely. Peel, wash and chop the onions. Wash and chop coriander leaves and mint leaves.
3. Mix chopped onions, chopped coriander and mint leaves with lemon juice to make a stuffing. Divide into sixteen equal portions and keep aside.

4. Heat two tablespoons of oil in a pan and add cumin seeds, coriander seeds, peppercorns, black cardamoms, stir-fry for half a minute on medium heat. Add chopped ginger, garlic and red chilli powder.
5. Add chicken *kheema* and *chana dal*. Add two cups of water and bring to a boil. Reduce heat and cook covered till *chana dal* is completely cooked. Cook on high heat to dry out the mixture completely, stirring continuously.
6. Remove from fire and cool. Grind chicken and *chana dal* mixture to a smooth consistency.
7. Add *garam masala* powder, mace and green cardamom powder and salt.
8. Mix well and check the seasoning.
9. Divide into sixteen equal portions. Flatten one in the palm of your hand and place a portion of onion stuffing in the centre. Shape into roundels and flatten slightly. Similarly shape the rest of the chicken mixture and stuffing.
10. Shallow fry till golden brown.
11. Serve hot with onion *lachcha* and Coriander and Mint Chutney.

Note: Refer page no. 101 for the recipe of Coriander and Mint Chutney.

> **CHEF'S TIP**
>
> If the chicken mixture is too moist after cooking, add roasted *besan* or powdered roasted *chana dal* as per your requirement.

TEX MEX CHICKEN WINGS

INGREDIENTS

Chicken wings	12-16	Worcestershire sauce	2 tbsps
Garlic	5-6 cloves	Tomato puree	¼ cup
Celery	2 inch stem	Tomato ketchup	¼ cup
Oil	1 tbsp	Red chilli powder	1 ½ tsps
Bay leaf	1	Peppercorns (crushed)	½ tsp
Brown sugar	1 tbsp	Salt	to taste
Malt vinegar	2 tbsps		

METHOD OF PREPARATION

1. Clean, wash and remove skin from chicken wings. Pat them dry with a clean and absorbent kitchen towel.
2. Peel and pound garlic along with washed celery stem to a paste.
3. Mix rest of the ingredients with the garlic and celery paste and marinate the wings for about one to two hours.

4. Preheat the oven to 200°C. Remove bay leaf from the marinade. Arrange chicken wings on the grilling tray of the oven. Ensure that the wings are placed in a uniform pattern to ensure proper cooking.
5. Cook for fifteen to twenty minutes at 200°C. Turn over the wings a couple of times, basting it with the remaining marinade.
6. Cook till it is crisp from outside, but soft and tender inside.
7. Serve hot straight from the oven.

CHETTINAAD FRIED CHICKEN

INGREDIENTS

Chicken .... 1 medium sized	Curry leaves 10-12
Onions .... 2 medium sized	Turmeric powder .... ½ tsp
Ginger .... 1 inch piece	Lemon juice .... 1 tbsp
Garlic .... 4-6 cloves	Rice flour .... 2 tbsps
Green chillies 4	Salt .... to taste
Red chillies whole 4-6	Oil .... to shallow fry

METHOD OF PREPARATION

1 Clean, wash and slit chicken through the backbone and the breast, into two equal halves. Make three to four half inch deep cuts on the breast and leg pieces.

2 Peel, wash and roughly chop onions, ginger and garlic. Remove stems and wash green chillies. Grind onions, ginger, garlic, green

chillies and red chillies, adding a little water if required. Wash, drain and finely shred curry leaves.

3. Blend turmeric powder, lemon juice and rice flour into the *masala* paste and mix in salt to taste.
4. Apply this mixture thoroughly and liberally on the chicken and leave to marinate for two to three hours, preferably in the refrigerator. Mix in shredded curry leaves into the chicken.
5. Heat oil in a shallow pan, add marinated chicken and sauté for two minutes on both sides to seal the exterior.
6. Reduce heat to medium, cover with a lid and cook for fifteen to twenty minutes, turning over and basting frequently with the remaining marinade. Sprinkle a little water if the chicken starts drying.
7. The last few minutes of the cooking should be done on high heat, so that the surface of the chicken is crisp and golden brown.
8. Cut into smaller pieces and serve hot.

BRANDY SPIKED CHICKEN

INGREDIENTS

Chicken breasts (boneless) 2	Chicken stock .... ½ cup
Red capsicum ... ½ medium sized	Oil .... 3 tbsps
Green capsicum .... ½ medium sized	Rosemary (dry) .... ½ tsp
Yellow capsicum .... ½ medium sized	Salt .... to taste
Asparagus 6-8	White pepper powder .... ¼ tsp
French beans 5-6	Worcestershire sauce .... 2 tbsps
Corn starch .... 1 tbsp	Brandy .... 3 tbsps

METHOD OF PREPARATION

1. Clean, wash, pat dry and cut chicken into quarter inch thin strips. Wash, halve and de-seed all the three peppers, cut them into quarter inch thin strips.

2. Wash, string and cut beans into one and half-inch sized pieces. Wash and cut the asparagus heads. Blanch (put in boiling water for few minutes and remove) French beans and asparagus and keep aside.
3. Dissolve corn starch in chicken stock.
4. In a pan take half the oil and sauté the chicken strips with rosemary on high heat for two to three minutes, season well. Remove and keep aside.
5. In the same pan add the remaining oil and toss all the vegetables for two to three minutes, season well. Remove and keep aside.
6. Make a mixture of worcestershire sauce and brandy and add to the pan. Add chicken, vegetables and cook on high heat.
7. Add the dissolved corn starch and cook for another two minutes or till the sauce thickens.
8. Serve hot.

Note: Refer page no. 103 for the recipe of Chicken Stock.

CHICKEN SATAY

INGREDIENTS

Chicken breasts (boneless) .... 4 medium sized

For marination
Lemon juice .... 2 tbsps
Dark soy sauce .... 1 tbsp
Oil.. 1 tsp
Red chilli powder................ 1 tsp
Salt .... to taste

For sauce
Peanuts (roasted) .... ¼ cup

Onion .... 1 small sized
Tomato puree .... 3 tbsps
Dark soy sauce .... 1 tbsp
Honey .... 2 tsps
Garlic .... 4 cloves
Salt .... to taste
Red chilli powder .... ½ tsp
Oil .... 1 tsp

METHOD OF PREPARATION

1 Clean and remove skin from chicken breasts, wash them and then cut each into half-inch broad strips. Slightly flatten these long chicken strips.

Chicken Satay

2. Mix all the marinade ingredients thoroughly, add flattened chicken strips to it and leave aside for an hour.
3. Thread marinated flattened chicken strips equally onto eight-inch long wooden skewers.
4. Heat a non-stick flat *tawa*, grease it slightly with a few drops of oil and place skewered chicken, a few at a time. Cook on high heat, turning them frequently. Cook for about three to four minutes or till it is just cooked.
5. Alternatively cook in a preheated grill for ten to twelve minutes or until done, turning them a couple of times.
6. Meanwhile prepare the sauce by peeling and grating onion. Peel and chop garlic. Crush roasted and peeled peanuts to a coarse powder.
7. Heat oil in a pan, add chopped garlic and grated onion. Cook on high heat, stirring continuously, for half a minute.
8. Add red chilli powder and then immediately add dark soy sauce, tomato puree, honey, crushed roasted peanuts, salt and one cup of water.
9. Bring it to a boil and simmer for five minutes, stirring occasionally.
10. Serve chicken satay accompanied with Peanut sauce.

> **CHEF'S TIP**
>
> Soak wooden skewers in water for half an hour, prior to cooking, to avoid the skewers from burning while cooking. This is helpful especially in open fire cooking or grilling.

ANDHRA CHILLI CHICKEN

INGREDIENTS

Chicken .... 1 medium sized	Red chillies whole 8-10
Salt .... to taste	Rice .... 2 tbsps
Lemon juice .... 4 tbsps	Yogurt .... ½ cup
Ginger .... 2 inch piece	Fresh coriander leaves ...... ½ cup
Garlic .... 6-8 cloves	Oil .... ¼ cup
Curry leaves 8-10	Refined flour .... ¼ cup

METHOD OF PREPARATION

1 Clean, wash and cut the chicken into four — two leg pieces and two breast pieces. Make four to five half inch deep slits on the pieces. Apply salt and two tablespoons of lemon juice and keep aside.
2 Peel and wash ginger. Peel garlic. Wash curry leaves. De-stem red chillies.
3 Grind ginger and garlic with curry leaves, red chillies and rice to a smooth paste by adding the remaining lemon juice. Blend this

paste into the yogurt and whisk well to a smooth consistency. Add salt to taste.

4. Apply this yogurt mixture liberally on the chicken pieces and leave to marinate for four to six hours, preferably in the refrigerator. Clean, wash and finely chop fresh coriander leaves.
5. Heat oil in a pan, roll the marinated chicken pieces in refined flour, shake the excess flour and shallow-fry. Cook for one minute, turn over the chicken pieces and cook for another minute.
6. Reduce heat and cook for five to six minutes, turning the chicken pieces frequently for uniform cooking. Remove and drain the chicken.
7. Transfer the chicken to a shallow pan and keep on medium heat. Sprinkle chopped coriander leaves and two tablespoons of water; cover with a fitting lid. Reduce heat and cook for five minutes on low heat or until the chicken is completely cooked.
8. Serve hot.

BARBECUED CHICKEN

INGREDIENTS

Chicken ....1 (800 gms)	Mustard powder................... 1 tsp
For barbecue sauce	Brown sugar........................ ½ cup
Onions................ 2 medium sized	Vinegar .... ¼ cup
Garlic .... 2 cloves	Worcestershire sauce .... 2 tbsps
Butter .... 4 tbsps	Pepper powder .... ¼ tsp
Tomato ketchup................. 1 cup	Red chilli powder .... ½ tsp
Chilli sauce .... ¼ cup	Salt .... to taste

METHOD OF PREPARATION

1 Skin, wash and clean the chicken. Make incisions with a sharp knife on the breast and leg pieces.
2 Peel, wash and finely chop one onion, cut the other into roundels and then separate the rings, keep the onion rings in chilled water to make them crisp. Peel and crush the garlic.

3. Heat two tablespoons of butter in a pan, add finely chopped onions and crushed garlic and fry till translucent.
4. Combine the remaining barbecue sauce ingredients and simmer over a low heat for ten minutes. Mix well. Allow it to cool. Keep aside a little quantity to serve with the cooked chicken.
5. Apply the remaining sauce to the chicken and let it stand for about an hour in a refrigerator.
6. Cook the chicken in a preheated oven (180°C) for ten to twelve minutes or until almost done. Baste it with the remaining butter and cook for another four minutes.
7. Serve hot with crisp rings of onion and barbecue sauce.

CHILLI CHICKEN

INGREDIENTS

Chicken (boneless) .... 400 gms	Garlic .... 8-10 cloves
Eggs 2	Green chillies 6-8
Cornstarch .... 2½ tbsps	Capsicums .... 2 medium sized
Salt .... to taste	Oil .... 1 tbsp + to deep fry
Soy sauce .... 2 tbsps	Vinegar .... 2 tbsps
Chilli sauce .... 2 tbsps	Ajinomoto .... ¼ tsp
Onions .... 2 medium sized	Peppercorns (crushed) .... ½ tsp

METHOD OF PREPARATION

1. Wash, trim and cut boneless chicken into finger sized pieces. Mix eggs, two-tablespoons of cornstarch, salt to taste, one tablespoon each of soy sauce and chilli sauce into the chicken pieces. Leave aside for half an hour.

Non-Vegetarian Snacks and Starters

2. Peel onions, wash, halve and cut into thick slices. Peel and finely chop garlic. Wash, remove stems and chop green chillies. Wash, halve, deseed and cut capsicums into thick strips. Blend half a tablespoon of cornstarch in three tablespoons of water.
3. Heat sufficient oil in a wok and deep-fry the marinated chicken pieces till crisp. Remove and drain on an absorbent kitchen towel.
4. Heat one tablespoon of oil in a wok or a pan, add garlic and stir-fry briefly. Add onion and green chillies. Continue to stir-fry for a couple of minutes.
5. Add the capsicum strips and sauté. Add remaining soy sauce and chilli sauce, ajinomoto, salt, crushed peppercorns, vinegar and blended cornstarch.
6. Add the fried chicken pieces and sauté till the sauce coats the chicken pieces.
7. Serve hot with Sichuan sauce.

Note: Refer page no. 99 for the recipe of Sichuan Sauce.

CHICKEN FLOWER DUMPLING

INGREDIENTS

Chicken mince	300 gms	Ginger	1 inch piece
Basmati rice	¾ cup	Salt	to taste
Green chillies	2-3	Peppercorns (crushed)	1 tsp

METHOD OF PREPARATION

1. Pick, wash and soak rice in water for twenty minutes. Drain and keep aside.
2. Wash green chillies, remove stem and chop them fine.
3. Peel and wash ginger. Grind into a fine paste.
4. Mix chicken mince with chopped green chillies, ginger paste, salt and crushed peppercorns. Divide this mixture into twelve equal portions.

5. Form round balls from each portion of chicken mix and then roll them in presoaked rice.
6. Place rice coated chicken balls on a perforated rack which can be fitted into a steamer pot.
7. Boil water in the steamer pot and place the perforated rack in it. Cover the pot.
8. Steam for about fifteen to twenty minutes or until cooked.
9. Remove gently and serve hot with a dip of your choice.

CHEF'S TIP

Chicken Flower Dumplings are made best with chicken mince that is extra fine, preferably from chicken breast only.

Chicken Flower Dumpling

CHICKEN CUTLET A L' INDIENNE

INGREDIENTS

Chicken breasts (boneless) 4	Eggs 2
Onion .... 1 medium sized	Cream .... 3 tbsps
Green chillies 2-3	Refined flour (*maida*) .... 1 cup
Fresh coriander leaves .. few sprigs	Breadcrumbs .... 1 cup
Salt .... to taste	Pepper powder .... ½ tsp
Peppercorns (crushed) .... ½ tsp	Oil .... to shallow fry

METHOD OF PREPARATION

1. Wash, clean and mince breasts of chicken.
2. Peel, wash and finely chop onion. Remove stems, wash and chop green chillies. Wash and chop coriander leaves.

3. In a bowl mix minced chicken with onion, green chillies, coriander leaves, salt and crushed peppercorns. Keep aside for twenty minutes.
4. Beat eggs in a large bowl with the cream.
5. Season flour and breadcrumbs with salt and pepper powder and keep in medium sized plates separately.
6. Take chicken mix and shape into cutlets. The shape could be round, oval, heart, tear drops, etc.
7. Coat the cutlets with the seasoned flour, remove excess flour, dip them in the cream and egg mixture and finally coat with the seasoned breadcrumbs.
8. Heat oil in a non stick frying pan and shallow fry the cutlets on medium heat on both sides till they are golden brown in colour and cooked.
9. Remove on kitchen towel or tissue paper to remove excess oil and serve hot.

ANDA AUR METHI PAKORA

INGREDIENTS

Eggs 8	Garam flour (*besan*) .... 3 tbsps
Fresh coriander leaves ...... ½ bunch	Carom seeds (*ajwain*) .... ¼ tsp
Fenugreek leaves (*methi saag*) ... . 1 cup	Red chilli powder .... ½ tsp
	Chaat masala .... 1 tsp
Onion .... 1 large sized	Cumin powder .... ½ tsp
Ginger .... 2 inch piece	Cooking soda .... ¼ tsp
Green chillies 4-5	Salt .... to taste
Spring onions 3	Oil .... to deep-fry

METHOD OF PREPARATION

1   Boil water and cook eggs for about ten to twelve minutes or till they are hard-boiled. Drain and immediately put into cold water. Remove shells and chop finely.

2. Clean, wash and finely chop fresh coriander and *methi saag*. Peel and finely chop onion and ginger. Wash, remove stems and finely chop green chillies. Wash, trim and finely chop the spring onions, along with the leaves.
3. Mix chopped *methi saag*, fresh coriander leaves, onion, ginger, green chillies and spring onions. Sprinkle *besan* and mix well. Add *ajwain*, red chilli powder, *chaat masala*, cumin powder, cooking soda and salt.
4. Add chopped boiled eggs, sprinkle a little water and mix to combine all the ingredients well.
5. Heat oil in a *kadai*, wet a tablespoon, scoop the egg mixture and gently drop into the hot oil. Fry the *pakoras* in small batches without overcrowding the *kadai*.
6. Cook for two minutes, turning the pakoras occasionally for even browning. Transfer the fried *pakoras* to an absorbent kitchen towel or paper.
7. Serve hot with tomato ketchup or Coriander and Mint Chutney.

Note: Refer page no. 101 for the recipe of Coriander and Mint Chutney.

CHICKEN GOLD COIN

INGREDIENTS

Chicken mince .... 250 gms	Cornstarch .... 2 tbsps
Onion .... 1 small sized	White pepper powder .... ½ tsp
Garlic .... 4-6 cloves	Ajinomoto .... ¼ tsp
Ginger .... ½ inch piece	Salt .... to taste
Green chillies 2-3	White bread .... 10 slices
Eggs 2	Sesame seeds (white) ...... 3 tbsps
Soy sauce .... 1 tbsp	Oil .... to deep-fry

METHOD OF PREPARATION

1 Mince chicken once again to get a smooth texture.
2 Peel, wash and finely chop onion. Peel and finely chop garlic. Peel, wash and finely chop ginger. Wash, remove stems and finely chop green chillies.

3. Add chopped onion, ginger, garlic, green chillies, one egg, soy sauce, cornstarch, white pepper powder, ajinomoto and salt to the chicken mince and mix thoroughly.
4. Break the remaining egg into a bowl, whisk lightly. Cut bread slices with a cookie cutter into one and half-inch diameter discs.
5. Brush bread pieces with whisked egg and apply a thick layer of the chicken mixture. Sprinkle sesame seeds generously on the prepared coins and press lightly. Shake off excess seeds and refrigerate for fifteen minutes.
6. Heat sufficient oil in a wok and deep fry the prepared gold coins for two minutes on high heat, stirring frequently. Reduce heat and fry further for three to four minutes or until crisp and golden brown in colour.
7. Remove, drain onto an absorbent kitchen towel and serve hot with a spicy and tangy sauce of your choice.

OPEN STEAMED DUMPLINGS

INGREDIENTS

Chicken mince	1¼ cups	Sesame oil	1 tsp
Green chillies	2	Salt	to taste
Spring onions	2	Peppercorns (crushed)	½ tsp
Ginger	1 inch piece	Wonton wrappers	16

METHOD OF PREPARATION

1. Wash, remove stems, deseed and finely chop green chillies. Wash, trim and finely chop spring onion along with the greens. Wash, peel and grind ginger into a paste.
2. Combine all the ingredients except the wonton wrappers in a mixing bowl. Cover with a cling wrap and refrigerate for half an hour.
3. Brush a wonton wrapper with a little water, place about two teaspoons of the prepared filling on it. Gather the edges together and squeeze

lightly to seal, leaving the top a little open.
4. Repeat the same with all the wonton wrappers, using up all the filling.
5. Arrange the dumplings in small batches in a steamer without touching each other and steam for about fifteen minutes or until the filling is cooked.
6. Serve hot with a hot and spicy sauce.

> **CHEF'S TIP**
>
> If you cannot get a Chinese steamer, use a cooker in the same way as you would steam *idlis* or *dhokla*.

PAPER WRAPPED CHICKEN

INGREDIENTS

Chicken breasts (boneless) ..... 300 gms	Soy sauce .... 2 tbsps
Red chillies whole 2-3	Sugar .... 1 tsp
Spring onions 8-10	Salt .... to taste
Ginger .... 1 inch piece	Egg 1
Five spice powder .... ¼ tsp	Rice/Butter paper ..... as required
Dry sherry (optional) ...... 2 tbsps	Oil .... for frying

METHOD OF PREPARATION

1 Clean, trim and cut chicken breasts into half inch sized pieces.
2 Soak red chillies in half a cup of hot water for ten minutes. Drain, remove stem and cut into julienne. Wash, trim and finely chop spring onions.
3 Peel and finely chop ginger. Mix chicken pieces with five spice powder, dry sherry, chopped ginger, red chillies, soy sauce, sugar,

Paper Wrapped Chicken

salt to taste and chopped spring onions. Rest the marinated chicken for an hour, preferably in the refrigerator.

4. Whisk egg with a pinch of salt and keep. Cut sixteen pieces of rice paper/butter paper measuring six-inches by six-inches.
5. Brush each piece of paper lightly with the whisked egg mixture and place two tablespoons of marinated chicken on one side of the paper. Drizzle some marinade on the chicken and roll tightly. Finally press or twist the two ends to seal.
6. Heat oil in a wok or deep pan and deep fry the paper wrapped chicken in hot oil for two to three minutes. Drain well and serve immediately, with a spicy sauce of your choice.

CHEF'S TIP

Let your guests unwrap the chicken on the table to savour the full aroma of the dish.

KHEEMA PAV

INGREDIENTS

Mutton mince .... ½ kg	Cloves 3-4
Onions .... 3 medium sized	Cinnamon .... 2 inch stick
Tomatoes .... 2 medium sized	Bay leaves 2
Ginger .... 1 inch piece	Red chilli powder .... 1 ½ tsps
Garlic .... 8-10 cloves	Turmeric powder .... ¼ tsp
Green peas (shelled) .... ½ cup	Cumin powder .... 1 tsp
Salt .... to taste	Coriander powder .... 1 tbsp
Fresh coriander leaves ... a few sprigs	*Garam masala* powder .... 1 tsp
Oil .... 3 tbsps	Butter .... 2 tbsps
Green cardamoms 3-4	*Pav* or bread rolls 8
Black cardamom 1	

METHOD OF PREPARATION

1. Peel, wash and finely chop onions. Wash and finely chop tomatoes. Peel ginger and garlic, grind to a fine paste.
2. Boil green peas in salted boiling water for five minutes or till almost

cooked. Refresh in cold water. Drain and leave aside.
3. Clean, wash and finely chop fresh coriander leaves
4. Heat oil in a thick-bottomed pan, add green and black cardamoms, cloves, cinnamon and bay leaves. Stir-fry briefly.
5. Add chopped onions and cook on medium heat, till they turn golden brown, stirring continuously. Add ginger and garlic paste and stir briefly. Add chopped tomatoes and cook till oil starts separating from the *masala*.
6. Add mutton mince and cook on high heat for three to four minutes, stirring continuously. Reduce heat, stir in half a cup of water and cook covered till mince is completely cooked. Stir occasionally.
7. Add red chilli powder, turmeric powder, cumin powder, coriander powder, salt and boiled green peas. Mix well and cook on high heat for a couple of minutes or till the mince is quite dry.
8. Sprinkle *garam masala* powder and garnish with chopped coriander leaves.
9. Heat butter in a thick-bottomed pan or a *tawa*. Slice *pav* horizontally into two and pan-fry in butter for half a minute, pressing two or three times or till *pav* is crisp and light brown.
10. Serve mince accompanied with pan-fried *pavs*.

CHICKEN TIKKA

Chicken breasts (boneless) .... 4 (600 gms)
Kashmiri red chilli powder .... 1 tsp
Lemon juice .... 1 tbsp
Salt .... to taste
For marinade
Yogurt .... 1½ cups
Kashmiri red chilli powder .... 1 tsp
Salt .... to taste

Ginger .... 2 inch piece
Garlic .... 8 - 10 cloves
Lemon juice .... 2 tbsps
Garam masala powder .... ½ tsp
Mustard oil .... 2 tbsps
Butter .... for basting
Chaat masala .... ½ tsp
For garnish
Onions .... 2 medium sized
Lemon .... 1 medium sized

METHOD OF PREPARATION

1 Clean and wash the chicken breasts. Pat them dry. Cut into two inch sized square pieces.
2 Apply a mixture of Kashmiri red chili powder, lemon juice and salt

and keep it aside for half an hour.
3. Peel, wash and grind ginger and garlic into a paste. Peel, wash and cut the onions into rings. Wash and cut the lemons into wedges.
4. Hang the yogurt in a muslin cloth for fifteen to twenty minutes so that the whey drains out. Mix Kashmiri red chilli powder, salt, ginger-garlic paste, lemon juice, *garam masala* powder and mustard oil with the yogurt.
5. Apply this mixture to the chicken pieces and keep in the refrigerator for three to four hours.
6. Put the chicken pieces onto skewers and cook in a moderately hot *tandoor* or a preheated oven (200°C) for eight to ten minutes. Baste with butter and cook for another two to three minutes.
7. Sprinkle *chaat* masala and serve with onion rings and lemon wedges.

KHEEMA FRANKIE

INGREDIENTS

Mutton mince (*kheema*) .... 1½ cups	Turmeric powder .... ½ tsp
Onions .... 2 medium sized	*Garam masala* powder .... 1 tsp
Tomatoes .... 2 medium sized	Salt .... to taste
Green chillies 2	*Chaat masala* .... 1 tsp
Ginger .... 1 inch piece	Coriander & mint chutney .. 4 tbsps
Garlic .... 3-4 cloves	**For the *roti***
Fresh coriander leaves ..... 2 tbsps	Refined flour (*maida*) .... ½ cup
Oil .... 2 tbsps	Whole wheat flour (*atta*) .... ½ cup
Red chilli powder .... 2 tsps	Salt .... to taste

METHOD OF PREPARATION

1. Clean and wash mutton mince and keep aside. Peel, wash and chop onions. Wash and chop the tomatoes. Remove stem, wash and chop the green chillies. Peel, wash and chop ginger and garlic. Wash and chop fresh coriander leaves.

2. Heat oil in a pan, add ginger, garlic, green chillies and stir fry briefly. Add half the onions and sauté for two to three minutes or till they turn golden brown in colour.
3. Add the minced meat, red chilli powder, turmeric powder, *garam masala* powder and cook stirring continuously till the mince is nearly cooked. Add tomatoes and salt and continue cooking for few more minutes. When the mince is completely cooked add coriander leaves, cover with a lid and remove from heat.
4. For the *roti*, sieve refined flour, whole-wheat flour and salt. Using sufficient water knead it into a soft dough. Cover it with a damp cloth and let it rest for ten minutes.
5. Divide into eight equal sized round balls. Roll out each ball into a thin *roti* of six inch diameter.
6. Cook *roti* on a hot griddle.
7. On each hot *roti*, place a portion of the cooked mince in the centre with some of the remaining chopped onion and Coriander and Mint Chutney. Sprinkle some *chaat masala* powder.
8. Roll the *roti* and seal the open edges with a toothpick. Serve hot.

Note: Refer page no. 101 for the recipe of Coriander and Mint Chutney.

CRISPY CHICKEN WONTONS

INGREDIENTS

Wonton wrappers 24	Garlic .... 4-6 cloves
Chicken mince .... ½ cup	Oil .... 2 tbsps + to deep fry
Cabbage .... ¼ small sized	White pepper powder .... ½ tsp
Capsicum .... 1 medium sized	Salt .... to taste
French beans 3-4	Ajinomoto .... ¼ tsp
Carrot .... 1 medium sized	Soy sauce .... 1 tsp
Spring onion 1	

METHOD OF PREPARATION

1. Wash, trim, remove core and finely chop cabbage. Wash, halve, deseed and finely chop capsicum. Wash, string and finely chop French beans. Wash, peel and finely chop carrot. Wash, trim and finely chop spring onion. Peel and finely chop garlic. Wash the chicken mince.

2. Heat two tablespoons of oil in a wok or a pan, add garlic and stir fry briefly. Add spring onion and chicken mince and sauté on high heat for three to four minutes. Add capsicum, French beans, carrot and cabbage and continue to stir fry for a couple of minutes more, stirring and tossing continuously.
3. Add white pepper powder, salt, ajinomoto, soy sauce and cook for half a minute. Remove and cool.
4. Divide prepared filling into twenty-four equal portions. Place a portion of the filling in the center of a wonton wrapper, wet the edges with a little water, fold into half diagonally, twist the ends and stick.
5. Repeat this process to prepare all the wontons. Heat sufficient oil in a wok, add prepared wontons and deep fry for two to three minutes or until crisp and golden brown in colour. Remove and drain onto an absorbent kitchen towel.
6. Serve hot with Sichuan sauce.

Note: Refer page no. 99 for the recipe of Sichuan Sauce.

Crispy Chicken Wontons

PATRANI MACHCHI

INGREDIENTS

Pomfret fillets 8	Garlic cloves 6-8
Salt .... to taste	Coconut (scraped) .... ½ cup
Lemon juice .... ¼ cup	Cumin seeds .... 3 tsps
Fresh coriander leaves .... 1 cup	Banana leaves 3-4
Green chillies 4	

METHOD OF PREPARATION

1. Clean, wash and cut fish fillets into two inch by one and a half inch sized pieces.
2. Sprinkle salt and half of the lemon juice and keep aside for half an hour.
3. Clean and wash coriander leaves. Remove stems and wash green chillies. Peel garlic.

4. Grind coriander leaves, green chillies, scraped coconut, cumin seeds and garlic to a fine paste. Add salt and remaining lemon juice to it. Mix well.
5. Apply this marination to the fish fillets and keep for at least fifteen minutes.
6. Wash and cut banana leaves into four pieces each. Pat them dry.
7. Put marinated fish pieces in the banana leaves along with a little of the marination and fold the banana leaves to cover the fish fillets completely. Repeat the same with all the fish pieces.
8. Steam the fish in a steamer for fifteen minutes and serve hot.

GOLDEN FRIED JUMBO PRAWNS

INGREDIENTS

Jumbo prawns 12-16	Ajinomoto .... ¼ tsp
Garlic .... 4-6 cloves	Salt .... to taste
Oyster sauce (optional) .. 2 tbsps	Refined flour (*maida*) .... ¾ cup
Lemon juice .... 1 tbsp	Cornstarch .... ½ cup
Soy sauce .... 1 tsp	Baking powder .... ¼ tsp
White pepper powder .... ½ tsp	Oil .... ¾ cup+to deep fry

METHOD OF PREPARATION

1 Wash, remove shell and devein prawns retaining the tip of the tail. Pat dry prawns thoroughly with an absorbent kitchen towel.
2 Peel and grind garlic to a fine paste.
3 Mix garlic paste, oyster sauce, lemon juice, soy sauce, white pepper powder, ajinomoto and salt to taste. Apply this mixture liberally

on the prawns and leave aside to marinate for two hours, preferably in the refrigerator.
4. Mix refined flour, cornstarch, baking powder, three-fourth cup of oil, salt to taste and three-fourth cup of water. Whisk thoroughly to make a batter of pouring consistency and set aside for twenty minutes.
5. Heat sufficient oil in a wok, dip marinated prawns in the batter by holding the tail and deep fry for two to three minutes on medium heat, turning frequently or until crisp and golden brown in colour.
6. Remove, drain onto an absorbent kitchen towel and serve hot with a sauce of your choice.

CHEF'S TIP

This batter needs to be whisked thoroughly so that the oil used in the batter is incorporated well. You can also increase the quantity of oil in the batter for crisper result.

GRILLED FISH FINGERS

INGREDIENTS

Fish fillets .... 400 gms	White pepper powder .... to taste
Lemon juice .... 3 tbsps	Dried thyme .... a pinch
Orange juice .... 4 tbsps	Worcestershire sauce .... 1 tbsp
Salt .... to taste	Whole wheat flour (*atta*) ...... ½ cup
Mustard paste .... ½ tsp	Oil .... 1 tbsp

METHOD OF PREPARATION

1 Clean, wash and cut fish fillet into finger sized pieces. Pat dry with a clean and absorbent kitchen towel.
2 Combine lemon juice, orange juice, salt to taste, mustard paste, white pepper powder, dried thyme and Worcestershire sauce thoroughly.
3 Mix the fish fingers in the above marinade. Refrigerate the marinated

fish fingers for about fifteen to twenty minutes.
4. Season whole wheat flour with salt and white pepper powder.
5. Roll marinated fish fingers in seasoned whole wheat flour. Shake off the excess flour.
6. Heat a non-stick *tawa*, lightly grease with a few drops of oil.
7. Place the fish fingers on it. Cook on medium heat, turning it occasionally for uniform cooking and colour. Cook till golden brown in colour.

> **CHEF'S TIP**
>
> Alternatively you may cook fish fingers in a preheated oven or a griller.

AMRITSARI FISH

INGREDIENTS

Boneless fish (preferably Surmai)	600 gms
Malt vinegar	½ cup
Gram flour (*besan*)	1 cup
Yogurt	½ cup
Egg	1
Carom seeds (*ajwain*)	1 tsp
Salt	to taste
Lemon juice	1 tbsp
Red chilli powder	1 tbsp
Ginger paste	2 tbsps
Garlic paste	2 tbsps
Oil	to deep fry
Chaat masala	1 tsp
Lemon wedges	6-8

METHOD OF PREPARATION

1. Clean, wash and cut fish into one and a half inch sized cubes. Marinate in vinegar for twenty minutes.
2. Remove from the vinegar and pat the fish dry.

3. Make a batter of *besan*, yogurt, egg, *ajwain*, salt, lemon juice, red chilli powder, ginger and garlic paste.
4. Keep the fish in this marinade for about twenty minutes.
5. Heat oil in a *kadai* and deep fry the fish till golden brown and crisp.
6. Serve hot, sprinkled with *chaat masala* and lemon wedges.

> **CHEF'S TIP**
> You could substitute malt vinegar with plain vinegar.

TANDOORI POMFRET

INGREDIENTS

Pomfret fish... 2 (300 gms. each)	Garlic paste .... 1 tbsp
Salt .... to taste	Carom seeds (*ajwain*) .... ½ tsp
Lemon juice .... 2 tbsps	Gram flour (*besan*) .... 2 tbsps
Yogurt .... ¾ cup	Turmeric powder .... ½ tsp
Egg 1	*Garam masala* powder .... 1 tsp
Ginger paste .... 1 tbsp	Butter/oil .... 2 tbsps

METHOD OF PREPARATION

1. Wash and clean pomfret fish. Make incisions on it and apply salt and lemon juice. Keep aside for twenty minutes.
2. Mix all the other ingredients except butter/oil. Apply this marinade to the fish and let it stand for about one hour in the refrigerator.
3. Put the fish on a skewer and cook it in moderate hot *tandoor* or pre-heated oven (180°C) for about eight to ten minutes.
4. Baste with butter and cook in *tandoor*/oven for another three minutes.
5. Serve hot with lemon wedges.

Tandoori Pomfret

PRAWN BALCHAO

INGREDIENTS

Prawns (shelled, headless) .... 600 gms	Mustard seeds....................... 1 tsp
Ginger .... 2 inch piece	Malt vinegar .... 1 cup
Garlic .... 15-20 cloves	Onions .... 2 large sized
Cumin seeds .... 1 tsp	Tomatoes (red) .... 4 large sized
Red chillies whole 12-15	Oil .... ¾ cup
Cloves 10-12	Sugar .... 2 tbsps
Cinnamon .... 2 inches	Salt .... to taste

METHOD OF PREPARATION

1. Devein the prawns. Wash and remove excess water. Add salt and keep aside.
2. Peel, wash and roughly chop ginger and garlic.
3. Grind ginger, garlic, cumin seeds, red chillies, cloves, cinnamon

and mustard seeds along with vinegar into a fine paste.
4. Peel, wash onions and chop them finely. Wash and chop tomatoes.
5. Heat oil in a *kadai* and sauté the prawns till all the moisture dries up. Remove prawns and keep aside. In the same oil sauté onions till they are soft and light brown. Add chopped tomatoes and cook on high heat till it forms a thick pulp and oil separates from the *masala*.
6. Add the ground spices and stir fry for two to three minutes. Add the prawns and sugar. Check seasoning and cook on low heat for another five to seven minutes or till oil separates from the *masala*.
7. Serve hot with bread or boiled rice.

> **CHEF'S TIP**
>
> You need not use large sized prawns for this dish as Prawn Balchao tastes better with small sized prawns and it is cheaper too !

ORIENTAL FISH KABABS

INGREDIENTS

For Kabab
Fish fillet	500 gms
Lemon juice	1 tbsp
Fresh button mushrooms	16
Fresh lychees	12
Black grapes (seedless)	24
Oil	½ tbsp

For Sauce
Ginger	1 inch piece
Garlic	2 cloves
Oil	1 tbsp
Soy sauce	2 tbsps
Peppercorns (crushed)	1 tsp
Red wine (optional)	2 tbsps
Honey	2 tsps

METHOD OF PREPARATION

1. Clean the fish fillets and cut it into twenty four equal sized cubes. Apply lemon juice and keep aside.
2. Wash and cut the stems of mushrooms. Sweat the trimmed mushrooms in one cup of water in a non-stick saucepan on medium heat with a lid on for three to four minutes. Toss them

occasionally. Remove, strain and keep the mushrooms aside and reserve the cooking liquor for the sauce.
3. Peel the lychees, halve, remove stone and keep aside. Wash the grapes and keep aside.
4. Peel, wash and finely chop the ginger. Peel and crush the garlic.
5. Heat oil in a small non-stick pan over moderate heat, add crushed garlic and chopped ginger to the pan and cook for fifteen seconds on medium heat. Add the soy sauce, crushed peppercorns, reserved cooking liquor, red wine and one fourth cup of water and bring to boil. Add honey and mix well.
6. Lower the heat and simmer gently for two to three minutes. Remove and keep warm till the kababs are ready.
7. Skewer fish, cooked mushrooms, black grapes and lychees on to the wooden skewers.
8. Brush with oil and grill for ten minutes. Alternatively cook in a pre-heated oven (180°C) for ten to twelve minutes or until the fish is tender. You can also cook this dish on a griddle plate or a thick pan. Use a non-stick pan for better results. Make sure to turn the skewers at regular intervals for even cooking.
9. Lace the kababs with the sauce and serve immediately.

CREOLE KING FISH

INGREDIENTS

King fish .... 4 one inch thick slices	Dried oregano leaves .... ½ tsp
Tomatoes .... 4 medium sized	Dried basil leaves .... ¼ tsp
Garlic .... 6-8 cloves	Dried thyme leaves .... ¼ tsp
Onion .... 1 medium sized	Tobasco sauce .... 1 tsp
Green chilli 1	Salt .... to taste
Fresh coriander leaves ...... ¼ cup	Oil .... 1 tsp
Lemon juice .... 2 tbsps	

METHOD OF PREPARATION

1. Wash and roughly chop two tomatoes and puree the rest in a blender. Process until nearly smooth. Set aside.
2. Peel and finely chop garlic. Peel, wash and slice the onion. Wash, remove stem and break green chilli into two. Wash and roughly chop fresh coriander leaves.

3. Wash fish slices and pat dry with a clean and absorbent kitchen cloth. Apply lemon juice and keep aside for five to ten minutes.
4. Cook chopped tomatoes, pureed tomatoes, sliced onion, chopped garlic, green chilli and one cup water in a non-stick sauce pan over medium heat for five to seven minutes, stirring frequently.
5. Reduce heat and stir in dried herbs, Tobasco sauce and salt. Cook for three to four minutes, or until liquid is reduced and sauce thickens, stirring frequently. Remove from heat and stir in chopped coriander leaves. Cover to keep warm.
6. Heat a non-stick pan, brush it with oil and place King fish slices. Cook on medium heat, turning once, for four to six minutes, or until fish is firm and opaque and just begins to flake.
7. Serve each fish slice topped with about three tablespoons of the prepared Creole style sauce.

PRAWN SHASLIK WITH APPLE CURRY SAUCE

INGREDIENTS

Prawns (peeled, deveined) .... 12-16 medium sized
Curry powder .... 1 tsp
Peppercorns (crushed) .... 1 tsp
Salt .... to taste
Lemon juice .... 2 tbsps
Capsicums .... 2 medium sized
Tomatoes .... 2 medium sized
Onions .... 2 medium sized

For sauce
Onion .... 1 medium sized
Ginger .... 1 inch piece
Green apples ..... 2 medium sized
Lemon juice .... 1 tbsp
Oil .... 1 tbsp
Bay leaf 1
Curry powder .... 2 tsps
White pepper powder .... ¼ tsp
Salt .... to taste

METHOD OF PREPARATION

For shaslik

1 Wash and pat dry the prawns and marinate them in curry powder,

crushed peppercorn, salt and lemon juice and refrigerate until required.
2. Wash, halve, deseed capsicums and cut into one inch sized square pieces.
3. Wash and cut the tomatoes in quarters, deseed and cut each quarter into two.
4. Peel and cut onions into quarters and separate onion segments.
5. Mix capsicums, tomatoes and onion pieces with the marinated prawns and refrigerate for fifteen to twenty minutes.
6. Skewer the marinated prawns and vegetables on a eight inch wooden skewer one after the other.
7. Heat a non-stick *tawa*, brush with a little oil and place the skewered prawns. Cook them on medium heat, turning occasionally, for five to six minutes or till prawns are just done. Serve hot topped with apple curry sauce.

For sauce
1. Peel, wash and roughly chop onion and ginger.
2. Wash, core and roughly chop the green apples. Mix the apple with lemon juice to prevent discoloration.
3. Heat oil in a non-stick pan, add bay leaf, chopped onion and ginger.

Cook on high heat, stirring continuously, for three to four minutes or till it just starts turning brown.
4. Add chopped green apples with one cup of water and boil.
5. Reduce heat and simmer for five to six minutes or till the apples are cooked and soft.
6. Add curry powder, white pepper powder and salt to taste. Cool, remove the bay leaf and puree the apple mixture. Pass it through a sieve and keep warm.

Prawn Shaslik with Apple Curry Sauce

CHILLI FISH BHAJJI

INGREDIENTS

Fish fillets .... 4 medium sized	Salt .... to taste
Ginger .... 1 inch piece	Rice flour .... 1 tbsp
Garlic .... 4-6 cloves	Refined flour (*maida*) .... 1 tbsp
Green capsicums ... 2 medium sized	Gram flour (*besan*) .... ½ cup
Red chilli powder .... 1 tbsp	Cooking soda .... ¼ tsp
Lemon juice .... 2 tbsps	Oil .... to deep-fry

METHOD OF PREPARATION

1. Clean, trim and cut fish into fingers of approximately two and a half inches by half inch by half inch each.
2. Peel ginger and garlic, grind to a fine paste.
3. Wash, halve, remove seeds and cut capsicum lengthwise into half inch broad strips.

4. Mix ginger-garlic paste, red chilli powder, lemon juice and salt to a thick paste. Apply this spice paste uniformly on the fish fingers and the capsicum strips.
5. Mix rice flour, refined flour, gram flour, a little salt and cooking soda thoroughly. Add sufficient water to make a smooth batter of coating consistency. Ensure that no lumps are formed.
6. Take a piece of fish finger, sandwich between two strips of capsicum and secure with two wooden toothpicks.
7. Heat oil in a *kadai*, dip the prepared fish and capsicum in the batter, shake off the excess batter and slide into hot oil. Deep-fry on medium heat for two to three minutes, turning over frequently or until golden brown and crisp.
8. Drain and keep on an absorbent kitchen towel or paper. Serve hot with coconut *chutney* or tomato ketchup.

PRAWN VARUVAL

INGREDIENTS

Prawns (shelled) .... 12-16 medium sized	Red chilli powder .... 2 tbsps
Ginger .... 1 inch piece	Turmeric powder .... ½ tsp
Garlic .... 6-8 cloves	Salt .... to taste
Cumin powder .... 1 tsp	Rice flour .... 2 tbsps
Tamarind pulp .... 1 tbsp	Oil .... ¼ cup
	Lemon juice .... 1 tbsp

METHOD OF PREPARATION

1 Devein, wash and pat dry prawns with a clean kitchen towel. Peel ginger and garlic, grind to a fine paste.
2 Mix ginger-garlic paste with cumin powder, tamarind pulp, red chilli powder, turmeric powder, salt and rice flour and blend two tablespoons of oil in the mixture.

3. Marinate prawns in this mixture and leave aside for at least two hours, preferably in the refrigerator.
4. Heat oil in a pan, add the marinated prawns and cook for a minute on high heat. Turn over the prawns and cook for another minute. Reduce heat and cook for two to three minutes turning the prawns occasionally for uniform cooking.
5. Remove, drain on an absorbent kitchen towel or paper, sprinkle lemon juice on the cooked prawns and serve hot.

DRAGON SEAFOOD ROLLS

INGREDIENTS

For Pancakes
Refined flour (*maida*) .... ½ cup
Cornstarch .... ¼ cup
Salt .... a pinch
Eggs 2

For Filling
Shrimps (peeled) 8-12
Fish fillet .... 100 gms
Crabmeat .... 1 cup
Spring onion 1
Ginger .... ½ inch piece
Garlic .... 2 cloves
Green chilli 1
Egg 1
Oil .... 1 tbsp + to deep fry
Red chilli paste .... ½ tsp
Ajinomoto .... ¼ tsp
Soy sauce .... ½ tbsp
Vinegar .... 1 tbsp
Salt .... to taste
Bean sprouts .... ½ cup

METHOD OF PREPARATION

1 Whisk all the ingredients for the pancake together with enough

water to make a thin smooth batter. Strain and set aside for half an hour.

2. Clean, wash, de-vein and roughly chop the shrimps. Wash and cut the fish fillet into small dices. Roughly chop the crab meat.

3. Wash, trim and finely chop spring onion. Peel and finely chop ginger and garlic. Wash, remove stem, deseed and finely chop green chilli. Break an egg into a bowl and whisk lightly.

4. To make the filling, heat oil in a pan, add chopped ginger, garlic, green chilli and stir fry briefly. Add red chilli paste and chopped spring onion. Sauté for a minute and add the chopped crabmeat, chopped shrimps and diced fish fillet.

5. Sprinkle ajinomoto, soy sauce, vinegar and salt to taste. Mix well and cook till the filling dries up and starts sizzling. Remove, cool and mix bean sprouts.

6. Heat a non-stick pan and brush a little oil. Mix the batter well and pour a ladle full, swirl the pan to coat and pour back the excess batter. Cook on medium to low heat, till the pancake starts leaving the sides of the pan.

> **CHEF'S TIP**
>
> Vegetarians can replace the chicken patties with potato or *paneer* patties.

7. Remove the pancake carefully and cool. Repeat and make twelve pancakes.
8. Divide the filling into twelve equal portions. Place a portion of the filling at the lower end of the pancake and roll, while folding the sides along. Brush the edges with egg and seal tightly. Repeat with all the pancakes and keep the rolls ready.
9. Heat sufficient oil in a wok and deep fry the prepared rolls in moderately hot oil, turning the rolls frequently until crisp and golden brown in colour. Remove and drain onto an absorbent kitchen towel.
10. Serve hot with a dipping sauce of your choice.

CHEF'S TIP

You can substitute the seafood with any of your favorite meats or vegetables.

SAMOSA POTLI

INGREDIENTS

Refined flour (*maida*) .... 1 cup
Semolina (*rawa*) .... 2 tbsps
Salt .... to taste
Ghee .... ¼ cup
Minced mutton (*kheema*) .... 400 gms
Green chillies 3
Ginger .... 1 inch piece
Fresh coriander leaves ..... 2 tbsps
Oil .... 2 tbsps + to deep fry
Cumin seeds .... 1 tsp
Red chilli powder .... 1 tsp
Coriander powder .... 1 tbsp
Cumin powder .... 1 tsp
Yogurt .... ¾ cup
Garam masala powder .... 1 tsp

METHOD OF PREPARATION

1 Knead together *maida*, *rawa*, salt and ghee with warm water to make a stiff dough. Keep covered for thirty minutes. Divide the dough into twenty balls.
2 Wash, de-stem and chop green chillies finely. Peel and chop ginger. Wash coriander leaves and chop them fine.

3. Heat two tablespoons of oil in a *kadai* and add cumin seeds. When they start crackling slightly, add *kheema* and sauté till half cooked. Add a little water if required.
4. Add ginger, green chillies, red chilli powder, coriander powder, cumin powder and salt and mix well. Cover and cook on low heat for fifteen minutes. Add yogurt. Cook on high heat for ten minutes, stirring continuously, till the *kheema* is fully cooked and completely dry.
5. Sprinkle *garam masala* powder and coriander leaves and mix well. Cool. Divide into twenty portions.
6. Roll the dough balls into small puris (three inch diameter). Place a *kheema* portion in the centre. Apply a little water on the areas a little away from the edges and shape like a *potli* or *modak*. Seal by pressing them.
7. Deep fry in medium hot oil till golden brown. Drain onto an absorbent paper.
8. Serve with chutney of your choice.

Samosa Potli

CRUNCHY CORIANDER POMFRET

INGREDIENTS

Pomfrets fillets (boneless) .... 2 medium sized	Peppercorns 8-10
Fresh coriander leaves ...... ½ cup	Red chillies whole 3-4
Salt .... to taste	Thyme (dry) .... ¼ tsp
White pepper powder .... ¼ tsp	Oil .... for shallow frying
Lemon juice .... 1 tbsp	Refined flour (*maida*) ...... 4 tbsps
Coriander seeds .... 2 tbsps	Cornstarch .... 1 tbsp

METHOD OF PREPARATION

1. Wash, clean and cut each fillet into eight pieces. Wash and chop coriander leaves.

2. Marinate the fish fillets with salt, pepper and lemon juice for about half an hour.
3. Dry roast the coriander seeds, peppercorns and red chillies. Grind to a coarse powder. Add thyme to this spice-mix.
4. In a frying pan, pour enough oil for shallow frying and heat.
5. In a bowl mix the spice powder, chopped coriander leaves, cornstarch and refined flour. Coat the marinated fillets with the mixture and shallow fry on both sides until golden brown and crisp.

GARLIC MUSTARD PRAWNS

INGREDIENTS

Prawns .... 20 medium sized	Cream .... 3 tbsps
Spring onions 2	Tomato ketchup .... 2 tbsps
Garlic .... 6-8 cloves	Salt .... to taste
Butter .... 2 tbsps	Peppercorns (crushed) .... ¼ tsp
Mustard (coarsely powdered) .... 2 tbsps	

METHOD OF PREPARATION

1. Shell, devein and wash prawns well. Pat dry on a kitchen towel.
2. Clean, wash and finely chop the spring onions.
3. Wash and chop the greens of one spring onion. Peel, wash and chop the garlic cloves.

4. Heat butter in a pan, add chopped spring onions, garlic and sauté slightly.
5. Add mustard powder, stir and continue to sauté.
6. Add prawns, cream and stir.
7. Add tomato ketchup, salt, crushed peppercorns and stir.
8. Cook for about half a minute on high heat. Do not overcook the prawns.
9. Add the spring onion greens and immediately remove from heat.
10. Serve immediately with French or garlic bread.

CHICKEN BURGER

INGREDIENTS

Burger buns	4	Egg	1
Chicken mince	400 gms	Mayonnaise	4 tbsps
Onions	2 medium sized	Tomato ketchup	2 tbsps
Cucumber	1 medium sized	Mustard paste	1 tbsp
Tomatoes	2 medium sized	Salt	to taste
Lettuce	1 bunch	Oil	3 tbsps
Breadcrumbs (optional)	½ cup	Butter	2 tbsps
Peppercorns (crushed)	½ tsp	French fries	as required

METHOD OF PREPARATION

1. Peel, wash and slice the onions and cucumber, wash and slice the tomatoes. Clean, wash, shred and keep the lettuce leaves in ice water for some time to retain its freshness.
2. In a medium-sized mixing bowl, combine the chicken mince, breadcrumbs, salt, half of the crushed peppercorns and egg together.

3. Mix mayonnaise with tomato ketchup, mustard paste and season with salt and remaining crushed pepper.
4. Divide the mince mixture in four balls and flatten them to form thick patties. Keep the patties in the refrigerator for half an hour. The size of the pattie should be larger than the size of the bun in diameter as it will shrink on cooking.
5. Heat oil in a non-stick pan or *tawa* and shallow fry the chicken patties, till they are golden brown, on both sides.
6. Slit the burger buns in half, apply butter on each half and toast on a *tawa* or grill. Remove and place on a working top.
7. Apply mayonnaise mix to the shredded lettuce. Place the lettuce leaves on the base-half of the burger and over it place cucumber and tomato slices. Now place a chicken pattie and finally a slice of onion. Put the other half of the bun over and close. Repeat the process with the remaining buns.
8. Secure with wooden sticks across so the pattie is held within.
9. Serve hot accompanied with French fries.

Note: Refer page no. 98 for the recipe of Mayonnaise.

> **CHEF'S TIP**
> Vegetarians can replace the chicken patties with potato or *paneer* patties.

FARMHOUSE LETTUCE ROLL

INGREDIENTS

Iceberg lettuce .... 8 leaves	Chicken mince .... 300 gms
Garlic .... 10-12 cloves	Black bean sauce .... 1 tbsp
Onion .... 1 medium sized	Salt .... to taste
Melon seeds .... 1 tbsp	Sugar .... ½ tsp
Oil .... 1 tsp	Peppercorns (crushed) ... to taste

METHOD OF PREPARATION

1. Wash iceberg lettuce leaves thoroughly and keep them in iced water.
2. Peel, crush and chop garlic. Peel, wash and finely chop onion. Dry roast melon seeds in a heated non stick pan till slightly browned.
3. Heat oil in a non-stick pan, add garlic and onion and cook till onion turns soft and translucent.

4. Add chicken mince and cook on high heat stirring continuously for about three to four minutes.
5. Stir in black bean sauce, salt, sugar and crushed black pepper. Mix well.
6. Cook covered on low heat till chicken mince is fully cooked. Remove from heat. Add roasted melon seeds and mix well.
7. Remove the lettuce leaves from iced water, shake off excess water. Arrange on a serving dish.
8. Put two spoonfuls of cooked chicken mince on each lettuce leaf and lightly roll and secure with a wooden toothpick. Serve immediately.

CHICKEN SEEKH KABAB

INGREDIENTS

Chicken mince (from the breast) .... ½ kg	Egg yolks 2
Fresh coriander leaves ...... ¼ cup	Salt .... to taste
Green chillies 2-3	*Garam masala* powder .... 1 tsp
Ginger .... 1 inch piece	White pepper powder .... 1 tsp
Garlic .... 4-6 cloves	Butter .... 2 tbsps
Cashewnuts 8-10	Lemon juice .... 1 tbsp
	Chaat masala .... 1 tsp

METHOD OF PREPARATION

1. Clean, wash and finely chop fresh coriander leaves. Wash, remove stems and roughly chop green chillies. Peel ginger and garlic, grind with chopped fresh coriander and green chillies to a fine paste without adding water.

2. Soak cashewnuts in warm water for ten minutes, drain and grind to a fine paste.
3. Blend ginger, garlic, coriander and green chilli paste with cashewnut paste and egg yolks. Mix this with chicken mince and add salt, *garam masala* powder and white pepper powder. Mix thoroughly and keep aside, preferably in the refrigerator for at least half an hour.
4. Divide the prepared chicken mixture into ten to twelve equal sized portions. Moisten your palms and spread each portion on to a skewer and shape them into *kababs* of four to five inches length.
5. Cook in a moderately hot *tandoor* for about eight to ten minutes turning them occasionally.
6. Brush the cooked *kababs* with butter and cook again for a minute in the *tandoor*.
7. They can also be cooked in a preheated oven at 220°C for about ten minutes. Brush the *kababs* with butter and cook for two minutes more.
8. Sprinkle lemon juice and *chaat masala* on the cooked *kababs* and serve hot.

MAYONNAISE

INGREDIENTS

Egg yolk	1	Sugar	¼ tsp
Salt	to taste	Vinegar	1 tsp
White pepper powder	¼ tsp	Oil	1 cup
French mustard powder	¼ tsp	Lemon juice	1 tsp

METHOD OF PREPARATION

1. Take a clean bowl. Place egg yolk, salt, white pepper powder, mustard powder, sugar and vinegar in it and mix it thoroughly with a whisk or hand or else transfer to a blender.
2. Add oil, a little at a time, whisking/blending continuously, until all the oil is incorporated.
3. Finish the sauce by adding lemon juice and adjust the seasoning.

SICHUAN SAUCE

INGREDIENTS

Green chillies 2	Oil .... ½ cup
Spring onions 2	Vegetable stock or water ...... ½ cup
Ginger .... 1 inch piece	Tomato ketchup .... 3 tbsps
Garlic .... 10 cloves	Salt .... to taste
Celery .... 2-3 inches stalk	Vinegar .... 2 tsps
Red chillies whole 10-12	

METHOD OF PREPARATION

1. Wash, de-stem and finely chop green chillies.
2. Peel, wash and finely chop spring onions. Wash and finely chop some of the spring onion greens.
3. Peel, wash and grate ginger. Peel and finely chop two cloves of garlic.
4. Wash and cut celery stalk into small pieces. Boil whole red chillies in one cup of water for five to seven minutes. Peel the remaining garlic.

5. Grind the whole red chillies and the remaining cloves of garlic to a fine paste.
6. Heat oil, add chopped garlic, green chillies, spring onions and ginger and sauté for a minute.
7. Add the red chillies and garlic paste and continue to sauté.
8. Add vegetable stock or water, celery, tomato ketchup, salt and stir to blend well. Add vinegar and spring onion greens.
9. Simmer for a minute and take off the heat. Cool and store.

CORIANDER AND MINT CHUTNEY

INGREDIENTS

Fresh coriander leaves	1 cup	Black salt	to taste
Fresh mint leaves	½ cup	Sugar	¼ tsp
Green chillies	2-3	Lemon juice	1 tsp

METHOD OF PREPARATION

1. Clean, wash and roughly chop the coriander and mint leaves.
2. Remove stem, wash, de-seed and chop the green chillies.
3. In a mixer, process chopped coriander and mint leaves with chopped green chillies. Make a smooth paste using a little water if required and remove. Add salt and sugar.
4. Remove in a bowl and mix in the lemon juice.

VARIATION

Add yogurt to the chutney and mix properly (one cup of yogurt for two tablespoons of chutney).

PEANUT YOGURT DIP

INGREDIENTS

Yogurt .... 2 cups	Red chillies whole 2
Peanuts (roasted) .... ¼ cup	Salt .... to taste
Fresh coriander leaves ..... 2 tbsps	Cream .... ¼ cup

METHOD OF PREPARATION

1. Hang yogurt overnight in a muslin cloth to remove excess moisture. This process can be carried out in the refrigerator to avoid the yogurt from getting too sour.
2. Wash and finely chop coriander leaves.
3. Crush roasted peanuts coarsely. Remove stem and crush red chillies.
4. Take yogurt in a mixing bowl, whisk it to get a smooth texture.
5. Season with salt, add crushed red chillies and peanuts and chopped coriander leaves. Whisk in the cream and mix well.

CHICKEN STOCK

INGREDIENTS

Chicken bones .... 200 gms.
Onion .... 1 medium sized
Carrot .... 1 medium sized
Celery .... 1 stalk
Leek 1
Parsley .... 2-3 stalks
Peppercorns 6-7
Cloves 5-6
Bayleaf 1

METHOD OF PREPARATION

1. Wash and clean bones, remove any excess fat. Heat sufficient water in a pan and put the bones in it and boil for five minutes. Drain and remove the bones.
2. Peel, wash and cut onion into quarters. Wash and cut carrot into three large pieces. Wash and cut celery, leeks and parsley stalks into two inch pieces. Wash leek leaves.
3. Put blanched bones, onion, carrot, celery, parsley, leek, leek leaves, peppercorns, cloves and bayleaf in a stockpot (deep pan) with ten

cups of water and heat. Bring the stock to boil, remove any scum, which comes on the top and replace it with more cold water. Simmer the stock for a minimum period of one hour.

4. Remove from heat, strain, cool and store in a refrigerator till further use.

GREAT OFFERS FROM THE KHAZANA OF MASTER CHEF SANJEEV KAPOOR

"My books are not simply a collection of recipes but an attempt to encourage people to cook ...and cook with confidence."

Khazana Of Indian Recipes
MRP: Rs 250/-

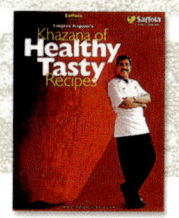

Khazana Of Healthy Tasty Recipes
MRP: Rs 250/-

Khana Khazana Celebration of Indian Cooking
MRP: Rs 250/-

BUY NOW

Low Calorie Vegetarian Cookbook
MRP: Rs 250/-

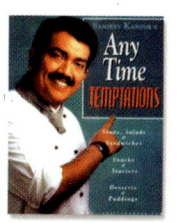

Any Time Temptations
MRP: Rs 225/-

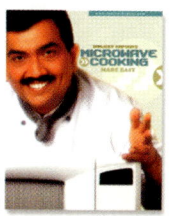

Microwave Cooking Made Easy
MRP: Rs 250/-

Best of Chinese Cooking
MRP: Rs 250/-

Subscribe to the most acclaimed food sites
www.sanjeevkapoor.com
and avail of unbelievable offers!!!

Pay **Rs. 500/-** only for one year subscription instead of normal subscription charges of **Rs. 1000/-** and get Sanjeev Kapoor Books worth **Rs. 750/- FREE** (only upto 31st January 2003).

You will also have access to more than 1000 recipes other than those published in his books besides many other sections, which will be a rare culinary treat to any food lover. In addition to online contests etc. you will also have opportunities to win fabulous prizes.

Sanjeev Kapoor also invites all food lovers to participate in the Khana Khazana Quiz and win BIG prizes every week. Watch Khana Khazana on Zee TV, answer one simple question based on that day's episode correctly, combine it with a favourite recipe of yours and you can be the lucky winner going places.

Subscribe to the most acclaimed food sites
www.sanjeevkapoor.com and avail of unbelievable offers

Normal Subscription	You pay	Plus you get	You save
Rs.1000	Rs.500	Sanjeev Kapoor's recipe books worth Rs.750	Rs.1,250

Offer open only upto 31st March, 2003

Great offer from the Khazana of Master Chef Sanjeev Kapoor.
Take your pick of book/books and avail of fantastic discounts.

Number of books	You save
1	Rs.25
2	Rs.100
More than two	Rs.200

Please tick the boxes below to indicate the books you wish to purchase

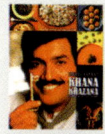

Khana Khazana Celebration of Indian Cooking	Khazana Of Indian Recipes	Khazana Of Healthy Tasty Recipes	Low Calorie Vegetarian Cookbook	Any Time Temptations	Microwave Cooking Made Easy	Best of Chinese Cooking
MRP: **Rs 250/-**	MRP: **Rs 250/-**	MRP: **Rs 250/-**	MRP: **Rs 250/-**	MRP: **Rs 225/-**	MRP: **Rs 250/-**	MRP: **Rs 250/-**
☐	☐	☐	☐	☐	☐	☐

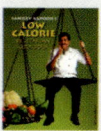

I'm enclosing cheque/DD No. _____ dated: _____ for Rs._____

(Rupees in words): _____ only drawn on

(specify bank) _____

favouring **POPULAR PRAKASHAN PVT. LTD.**, MUMBAI.

Name: Mr./Ms.

Address:

City: Pin: State:

Phone Res: Off: E-mail:

Please fill in the coupon in capital letters and mail it with your cheque/DD to
Popular Prakashan Pvt. Ltd.,
35-C Pt. Madan Mohan Malaviya Marg, Tardeo, Mumbai-400 034.
Phone: 022-24941656, 24944295 Fax:022-24945294 , E-mail: info@popularprakashan.com
www.popularprakashan.com

Delivery subject to realisation of cheque/DD. Offer valid in India only
Please allow two weeks for processing your subscription. Please superscribe your name and address on the reverse of the cheque/DD
All disputes are subject to the exclusive jurisdiction of competent courts and forums in Mumbai only